MRITYAA

ANURADHA IYER
SATISH PUROHIT

Made with ♥ on the Notion Press Platform
www.notionpress.com

Contents

Foreword

So beautiful... It is like reading The Gita. How consoling it is to know that one is never ever alone!! Even when the whole physical world is with you, or leaves you, MRITYAA is always with you till your last breath and gives you eternal peace in her lap when you breathe your last! Mesmerizing and comforting at the same time! Thanks, Radha/Mrityaa/Krishna, for the Teaser Trailer of the film we all will eventually see!! Just like the Bhagwat Gita, reading a page of this book every day, and the fear of death will be transformed into the excitement of going on an adventure reading a page of this book every day, and the fear of death will be transformed into the excitement of going on an adventure with God by your side! MRITYAA - A Treasure to keep and refer to, till your last breath! - **Dr. Neeraj Sethi (Pathologist, Educator, Spiritual philosopher, Musician, Mentor)**

"Iyer has personified death and its experience in a very approachable way. I enjoyed reading this engaging story and have taken away so many nuggets of wisdom. I encourage everyone to get to know Little Mrityaa and spend some quality time with her."- **Alka Dhillon (International Best Selling author of The OM Factor, Founder & CEO | Technalink, Inc)**

Every action is a seed that holds forests of consequences; nothing ever goes unrewarded or unpunished. Dr. Anuradha Iyer's book Mrityaa has taken on the dark and difficult subject of death and karmic redemption with childlike ease and mirth. This is straight-from-the-heart writing, at its honest best. We gently but firmly confront the transient nature of life and the inevitability of death, actually looking forward to the embracing arms of eternity. Beautiful.... - **Meena Iyer (Psychologist, Healer, Hypnotherapist,**

Reiki master, Philosopher, Musician, Mentor)

Growing up with my dear sister Anu (Dr Anuradha Iyer), I would have never imagined that one day she would write with such ease on the subject of death - something that has befuddled, eluded,, I would have never imagined that one day she would write with such ease on the subject of death - something that has befuddled, eluded, and scared the bravest of hearts. Last summer, when Anu visited me in Bangalore, she was writing the final drafts of this book, and, to our surprise, my Father read each word and discussed it with her and with all of us, to our surprise, my Father read each word and discussed it with her and with all of us with great interest. Little did we know that we would lose him in less than a month after that to the very same mystery. I believe Anu may have done just that little bit to help my Father face the inevitable with his characteristic grace and courage. For that, I will always be deeply grateful to Anu. To meet death in every living moment with a smile and a prayer is the best way to live - this message resounds deeply in our minds and hearts long after we finish reading Mrityaa...truly enlightening!-**Kavita Iyer (IITian, IIMian, Educationist, Musician, Mentor)**

A MOST ENCHANTING JOURNEY OR EXPERIENCE OF PASSAGE FROM LIFE TO DEATH N BEYOND... TO ETERNAL BLISS. The character of Mrityaa especially looks very real in a world of the unreal. Her encounters with Anuradha and others are kind of mysterious yet believable. Her encounters with Anuradha and others are kind of mysterious yet believable. Well written with a good mix of fiction and the Eternal Truth, that is, Death itself. Thoroughly enjoyed reading it.-**Sheela Iyer (Musician, Educationist, Philosopher, Mentor)**

Your spiritual journey has been phenomenal, and I, being a witness to it, can proudly share that I gained so much strength, solace, and, and I, being a witness to it, can proudly share that I gained so much strength, solace, and love in my life from your journey itself. And I am yet to offer my wholehearted gratitude to you for your warmth and loving friendship, which you always offered unconditionally. This book is as amazing and breathtaking as your first one. You have discussed in a simplified manner the journey to death. A cute Mrityaa. Our angel. Our lover. Our answers to all queries, ifs or buts. Our patient partner who witnesses the evolution of our soul. I would recommend this book for all age groups so that the basic mindset about death can be questioned and a new seed of thought can be sown in the fertile minds of every generation, who would then look at death with a can be questioned and a new seed of thought can be sown in the fertile minds of every generation, who would then look at death with a new outlook and more loving acceptance.- **Dr. Prakriti Vohra (Microbiologist, Philosopher, Healer, Tarot Reader, Educationist, Musician, Mentor)**

I am a Holistic Health Physician and have often pondered about death and the mystery behind life after death. Death is considered a taboo subject to most, but Dr. Anuradha Iyer, an extremely talented and creative writer and a spiritual human being, has portrayed death in such a beautiful way that once you pick up this book and start reading, you can't put it down till the end. Probing, passionate, and insightful, this is a must-read for all who fear death and are not willing to look it in the eye, which is most of us. The story will help you see death from a completely new perspective, which is at once mesmerizing and poignant. Those who might have recently faced the death of a loved one and might be in denial, anger, or depression may be consoled and be more accepting of it, and could feel a sense of closure. Overall, a must-read.- **Dr. Sanchita Bhattacharya (Holistic Health Physician, Author, Philosopher, Mentor,**

Educator)

Dr. Anuradha Iyer has taken Death by its horns, head-on, and has built up an option which emphasizes that death is neither dark nor deadly. It is the only truth of life. From the moment one is born, the only thing for sure is death. It is nothing morbid. Her articulation, sequencing & storyline are excellent. Must read for every student of life.- **Dr. PNN Iyer (Economist & Corporate Mentor. MBA & PhD Prof.)**

There have been signs. The graying of hair, the sagging of sinew, and the riverine wrinkles mapping the skin point towards the inevitable – death is near. This is not true just for me, but for all who are born. Eventually, all of us will pass. We are all, without exception, part of one uninterrupted procession on its way to the cremation grounds. If we believe we are going anywhere else, we are mistaken. For the embodied, death is destiny. Tending to our funeral pyres is Lady Time, or Kalika, the feminine of Mahakala, or Great Time. She awaits our return, for she is the mother who feeds our worn bodies into the funeral pyre. "Come home," she calls. "The sun is setting. Halt your play. Sleep in time so you awaken refreshed to a new day, a new dawn filled with learning, love, and play." The good news is that death is temporary. Life, on the other hand, is forever. I hope everyone will enjoy this tale rich in magic, metaphor, and life as much as I did and profit from it, too. Life is precious, whispers Mrityaa, because death is inevitable. - **Shivi Verma (Editor, Life Positive)**

Acknowledgements

This book is the result of my deep desire to write on the two-fold subject of living passionately and dying consciously. Every word in this book, which I have co-written with Satish Purohit, has been inspired by my beloved Krishna, to whom is dedicated this fruit of our combined effort.

I thank my parents, my son, my husband, my sisters and their families, my friends, my relatives, my colleagues, and all my well-wishers for making these beautiful insights possible for me. A special thank you to the illustrator, Mamta Shah, who read the thought behind my thought and the feeling behind my feeling and made the characters of the story come alive with the power of her magical brush. Thank you, loved ones.

I also thank my darling Mrityaa, who is always with me and whom I look forward to meeting in the sweetness of time.

Anuradha Iyer

CHAPTER ONE

BEYOND HIS PRESENCE

So, where do I begin the story of my Father? My life till two weeks ago was secure, good, happy, and I was loved. Today, I am bereft of something vital, his presence, his physical presence, not his consciousness, because that is alive, even while I write, it will always be alive...... forever!!!

I am writing this chapter on my father, and it is for a very special reason. Two weeks before he passed on, my father read my book Mrityaa, and we had a wonderful discussion about it. So, I feel that he has blessed this book and given me his approval and love to go on with its publication. He asked me what had motivated me to write about such a difficult topic, death. I told him I was passionate about understanding death and making it easy for people to face their own mortality and to allow their loved ones to pass on and continue their soul journeys. He asked me, "How do you know what happens to the soul after death?"

My Dearest Father

And I said, I really don't know, but I have an intuition about it, and I believe what I have read about it by other authors, and also from authors who have experienced NDEs. He was fascinated, for sure. He read the book twice, and I somehow feel, in retrospect, that Mrityaa helped Papa understand death and be prepared for it in some way. The day before he passed on, my father knew he was on his way out. He told me very clearly, please don't mourn my death, instead celebrate my life, for I have lived a full life and enjoyed every experience. I salute his spirit and his courage in facing death, and Papa is the winner, I know.

My earliest memories of my father are of this strong, smiling man, who poured out his love on my Mother, his Mother (my grandmother), and on us three girls, his daughters. So much love, so much genuine affection and caring, nobody has ever given me so much, and all without any expectations of any kind. I can feel only gratitude towards this amazing person, my father, whose words can never be described or limited.

I remember, when I was a little girl and when we would be out somewhere, walking back home, and I would be so tired and sleepy that I couldn't walk another step, then my father would carry me home and tuck me into bed very, very gently, as if I was the most precious bundle of joy he had, the feeling I had at those moments, was the safest, the most loved and cared for human being ever.

Throughout my childhood, my father never, ever raised his voice at any of us, children. He always spoke to us with utmost love and explained patiently, answering our doubts and questions, giving us his time, love, and encouragement ever so generously.

His greatest wish was for us to be compassionate human beings, to feel others' pain, and to heal them with love and care. He would narrate stories to us about Mother Teresa, Florence Nightingale, Tagore, and Mahatma Gandhi, always trying to instill in us the values of these wonderful human beings. He taught us how to enjoy reading from childhood.

In our summer vacations, Papa would take us to the local bookstore and buy us books, classics, written by the best authors in the World. He would discuss the books and stories with us and highlight the human values they convey. He would quote Shakespeare, William Wordsworth, and every famous poet and writer. Those were our most precious treasures.

My father inspired me to study medicine from a very young age. I don't know what he saw in me, but he felt I would be able to understand others' pain and, with my love, heal the World. He bought me the best books, so I could prepare for my entrance exams. The amazing thing was that he never put any pressure on me; it was always the motivation, the most inspiring stories, which made me want to study and do my best to clear the entrance exams for getting admission to Medical College.

I still remember the day he checked my results, the day they were declared, and came home with the newspaper cutting in his hand, after his morning walk. He rang the doorbell so many times that we thought it would break. I had cleared my entrance exams for the Madhya Pradesh PMT, and I would get admission to study at our Medical College in my hometown, Jabalpur. Papa was overjoyed, and I was happy in his happiness. I really wasn't so brilliant academically, but I guess I made it because of the determination he instilled in me to be one-pointed in my efforts and to make his dream a reality. This is something I still can do; whenever I make up my mind to do something, I don't give up until I do it successfully. The credit for this, of course, goes to my beloved Father.

Every decision in my life was always supported by my Father, regardless of whether he personally liked it. He would ask me a lot of questions to understand why I made any decision. He would talk to me about it, tell me the pros and cons, and explain the dangers and pitfalls, but he always gave me the freedom to decide what I wished to do. He trusted me to do the best for myself and my loved ones.

His freedom and trust mean more to me than anything else; that was the greatest expression of his love. It is rare for any parent to give their children freedom while also protecting them. Freedom to be myself, and yet always stand by me, so that if I ever fell, he would be there to pick me up and motivate me to go on. I love that so much!!!!

My father was the greatest inspiration for me to always be financially independent. He would explain in great detail to all of us daughters that financial independence for a woman was very, very important. He wanted us to be financially independent, so we could make our own decisions and not depend on others. This gave us a lot of confidence and the freedom of expression. It is only because of this freedom that I am able to fulfil my dreams and live a satisfactory life today.

For my Mother, though, he did not want her to leave home and work. In this decision of his, I can only see the great love and care he expressed for her, because he knew she was such a gentle woman, brought up in the most protected environment, and that she would not have been able to handle the big, bad world. He always spoke to me about it. Take care of your Mother after I leave, he told me, on more than one occasion. As if he knew that he would go before she did. And that one of our daughters would need to take care of Mom. We cannot even attempt to care for Mom as he did, but of course, we can only try our best. And all three of us will do our best, I know.

After Papa passed away, it's been thirteen days. I came back home with my mother, and the first thing I did was to read the last chapter of Mrityaa. I realized that I needed my own words to comfort me at this crucial juncture in my life. And believe me, O esteemed reader, it made a lot of sense to me. After his death, I had been in touch with him throughout. Every moment I have been receiving messages from him and talking to him, I actually feel closer to him in spirit than before.

Because he now knows me better, he is actually experiencing all my experiences, so he understands me much more. I understand him much more, because all those things we could never talk about in his life, when he was in form, body, and mind, we can share now, when he is conscious. My Father is Krishna now. He has merged with Krishna forever. And I can feel his love for me so clearly, so beautifully, so completely. I am blessed beyond comparison.

I found a notebook on his bedside table with his handwritten notes on various spiritual books he had read. It is profound; it is my most precious gift from him. I am going to make that a book which will be his precious gift to the World. I know from what he has shared in his notebook that his understanding of spirituality is very advanced, and I hope he has attained Krishna forever and will have no unfulfilled desires to return to Earth. Though he was very keen to make me a surgeon, and I couldn't be one. He just might return to Earth to heal others. One line which talks about this, those who see the Truth, never return to this World of Births and deaths except to enlighten other lives and bring light to all.

CHAPTER TWO

LITTLE MS. DEATH

The one who senses the footsteps of death is not even interested in eating, what to say of harming others. Those who mistakenly believe they will live forever commit evil acts.- Subhashita Manjari

The nine-year-old girl had wide eyes lined in kohl and a dimpled smile. "You don't remember me, do you?" she asked Anuradha. "Here, look at this picture. Isn't this you?" Anuradha was puzzled. She took the smartphone from the girl's hands and stared. The color picture was taken in a college in Kolkata way back in the 1820s, a decade before the advent of photography and nearly 200 years before the arrival of smartphones.

How did Anuradha identify the year with such certainty? How did she know that this woman, who looked so different from her, was herself in a different body? How was all of this even possible? Anuradha was clueless about how she knew, but she had no doubt that it was all true. And then it all came back to Anuradha in a flash. Of course, she knew who this little girl was. Here, when you had a body, she was Mrityaa or death. In the higher realms, she was Amrita, or immortality.

"Hey, you had promised me I would have a daughter like you in this birth. I wanted to raise that daughter with my own hands. Oil her hair with my hands and tie two tight ponytails in a flaming red ribbon," laughed the girl, finishing Anuradha's sentence for her. "Ah, Mritya, you are back. Is it time already? It must be," smiled Anuradha as she held the little girl's lovely head in her palms and kissed her forehead. Mrityaa laughed happily at the show of affection. "You may continue to wear this body for some more sunrises and some hours before it is time to leave," she smiled. "I came early so we could spend some time together." "And, why this special favor?" "Not a favor at all, Maa.

We had decided that we would meet some days before it was time for you to leave," said Mritya, her sweet face clouding with doubt. "Oh, you do remember that you wanted me to call you Maa, don't you?" "Yes, it is all coming back to me. So lovely of you to remember your promise," smiled Anuradha. "Where have you been?" "I have always been with you. I walk with every soul from the instant it inhabits a body till the very end when they discard it, but I am not allowed to reveal myself till the very end. " Mrityaa touched Anuradha's hand, and she felt her eyes grow a little wider as she looked around her and witnessed hundreds of little Mrityas following each person in the crowd. "Why would you, who are death, stalk the living?" asked Anuradha.

"Oh, that is because all of living is but dying in installments," explained Mrityaa. Anuradha felt a deep love for Mrityaa welling up, deep inside her. "So much wisdom in this little head, Mrityaa!" she teased. "Yeah, I know. Right?" Both of them began to laugh. They were so loud that hundreds of onlookers at the busy Chandni Chowk market stared at the sight of the old grandmother in her silk sari laughing with little Mrtitya. Little did they know! "Please share the joke," said a woman in her 40s in mock seriousness.

"What a pretty granddaughter you have!" "Shalini aunty, you will get it soon enough," smiled Mrityaa sweetly. "Everyone does. Eventually." The woman was flummoxed. "How do you know my name?" she asked. "I am in Moni's class at Aryavart Public School," said Mrityaa. "Oh!" the woman smiled. "I am flattered that you remember my name. Moni is the most popular girl in the class. Everyone knows you, Auntie," said Mrityaa, which pleased the woman.

Anuradha took Mritya's hand and started walking towards the car. "There is so much to do, and few days are all I have. Will just have to leave some things unfinished, I guess," said Anuradha wistfully. Mrityaa, ever full of answers, suggested she make a list of to-dos. "Ah, another list. My last!" smiled Anuradha. "I have made so many. They do not always help."

"This list will surely help. You have an important 'deadline' to meet," said Mrityaa. "Yes, a rather important 'deadline'!" laughed Anuradha, wondering if people would fear death as much as they did if they could meet this sweet girl. "But before you attend to anything else, I want to introduce you to a friend," said Mrityaa. "Look over there. There she is!" Anuradha looked out of the car, and her eyes beheld the strangest woman she had ever seen in her life. "Oh!" said Anuradha. "Who is this?" she hissed, trying not to be rude. They were at a deserted crematorium on a desolate stretch of road connecting Delhi and Gurgaon. On the wall surrounding the grey structure stood a buxom blue woman with a round face, blood-red lips, and hair that seemed to crackle with dangerous energy. She was naked except for an assortment of necklaces with fist-sized off-white beads.

Anuradha adjusted her spectacles to get a clearer look as the blue woman extended her hand, "Kalika. Smashan Kalika," she smiled sweetly. "Whaa..?" asked Anuradha. "Ha!" laughed Mrityaa. "Smashan Kalika, she is the body recycler." "Kalika! Kalika! Kalika!" repeated Smashan Kalika as she rolled her eyes. "Please call me Kali. I insist. No formality, okay? This is a place to chill out!" "Chill out, eh?" roared Mrityaa. Anuradha could not help but smile uneasily as Smashan Kalika winked at her. "I like doing the plump ones. The way the fat sizzles is awesome.

It was a low hum when it caught Anuradha's attention. She looked in the direction of the sound. It was a group of people of all ages, ranging from nine onwards. They were all stark naked. One of them, a man in his sixties whose face seemed familiar, coughed to attract Kalika's attention. "Mother," he said, "May I request something?" "Yeah, what is it?" asked Kalika, rolling her eyes again. "Can we have our bodies back?" he asked. "No, you can't," said Kalika."Okay, can I have my body back?" asked the man again. "No. No and No," said Kalika. "It has been returned to the elements. Now, if you just focus on the transition, you can leave this subtle body as well. It is all over, son." "Chill!" said Mrityaa as she put her hands on her mouth and tittered. "Mammals are funny, alright, but dead mammals, they are hilarious!"

Anuradha laughed at the joke. The ghosts noticed her. "Hey," said a pretty girl who appeared to be in her twenties. "How come she gets to keep her body? She is not even dead, and she is able to see all of us." "She sees us!" said a teenage girl. Smashan Kalika raised a hand to silence the ghosts. "Well, she's met death while she is still alive. She will leave her body consciously,"

A teenage girl with jet-black skin, four hands, and three eyes began to sing in a thin, melancholic voice as she strummed her guitar.

It is dusk, wind up your play
Hey kids, it's the end of the day
Mother says wash off the grime
of this playground of space-time
Come bathe in the pools of fire
Rid bodies soiled with desire
Of the five colors, is your little city
And of a million hues, infinity
From Mother we come, to Mother we go
That, my friends, is all there's to know

As she began her song, other beings with various instruments appeared, playing them all. The black girl began singing every line in seven different ways, and everyone, including the ghosts, started clapping. As the song reached a crescendo, many of the assembled beings began dancing. "Wow, Bhairavi! You have improved!" said Mrityaa after the girl was done singing. "Bhairavi has been practicing. She is trying to incorporate my name into the song," smiled Smashan Kalika.

The ghosts began their grumbling again. "Give us our bodies, Mother!' said an old woman. "Oh, shut up!" said Smashan Kalika. "You did not live well when you had bodies, and now you want the bodies back when you are dead. Quit grumbling and stay dead."

Anuradha noticed that the crowd had thinned somewhat. "Have some of these people left?" she asked Smashan Kalka. "Some of them have already taken birth," Kalika explained. "The music brought those sourpusses to the present, and they had let go of their past. They ceased being ghosts the moment they let go. You can't be a ghost if you don't dwell in the past. It is a rule!" "Whose rule?" asked Anuradha.

"Mine, of course. I am Lady Time. Kalika. I am in the moment. I am past. I am the womb of the future. I am eternity. I am also a lot of fun." Mrityaa said, "Yes, you are!"

Anuradha looked at her watch. It was getting late. "Oh, don't you worry," said Bhairavi. "Time stops for you when you are with Kalika. When you return, you will notice that you have not spent even a second here. I want to play another song for you. We just formed a band. We are one Gandharva short. You will do too if you are willing to hang around after you give up the body." The Gandharvas did not appear pleased with the suggestion. "What do humans know about music? Why would you even consider a human? I am feeling so disrespected right now," said one with flowing locks that reached his ankles.

All the Gandharvas looked crestfallen. "Pushpadanta, I am the leader of the band. I get to decide. She can do something simple in the beginning," said Bhairavi. "I would not mind that," said Neelambara. "Make her praise us while we play." Anuradha tried hard to suppress a smile. "You have not even asked me if I want to join the band," she said.

"Do not even think of ditching the band," said Bhairavi. "You will have the best time of your death with us. If you think life is beautiful, you should try death. It is super awesome."Mrityaa began to tug at Anuradha's hand. "Let us leave now. We can always return later," she said. "All right, folks! See you!" said Smashan

Kalika."Okay, guys. Let us belt one song for Anuradha. A goodbye song," said Bhairavi.

A Gandharva began beating his drum. Another flautist joined in, followed by another with huge cymbals the size of manhole covers. Bhairavi closed her eyes. Anuradha, goodbye, goodbye. Until three sunrises in the sky. Die early; do not be a pain. So long till we meet again. An remains in each other's hearts.Till LAAAEEEEFFFF do us part. The Gandharvas began clapping wildly. Anuradha saw the ghosts tap their feet to the song and disappear a moment later in a cloud of smoke. They had arrived in the moment and achieved freedom.

Mrityaa and Anuradha walked towards the car. As they drove away, Anuradha saw the beings waving at her. Smashan Kalika was back on her perch on the crematorium wall, with her long hair arranged all around her. There was a fresh batch of ghosts approaching her. Kalika looked at them, then at Anuradha, and rolled her eyes. Anuradha laughed at the now familiar gesture. Smashan Kalika winked in response. "Hey there! Hey there!" called out thousands of voices on both sides of the road. "Hey, Mrityaa!" Anuradha looked out to see hundreds of white apparitions chasing the car on both sides of the road.

"Is it true?" one asked as it flew so close that Anuradha could feel its cold breath smelling of mushrooms and cut grass. "Is it true that the new moon of this month ensures rebirth in a rich family?" "No," said Mrityaa. "Your deeds have already decided where you will be born. The full moon is just the time when souls destined to be reborn in rich families are dispatched into the world.

"Oh," sighed an apparition deep in the crowd of white that had grown to thousands now. "What is this woman doing walking around with a body and all?" "She's joining you shortly," said Mrityaa as she looked fondly at Anuradha. "Maa, sing for them." Anuradha was taken aback at the request. Sing? In the middle of nowhere for these beings? "Who are these people? Ghosts?" asked Anuradha. "No! No! No!" rose the deathly chorus. "Ghosts live in the past. We are futuras."

Anuradha looked at Mrityaa for an explanation. What on earth were futuras? "They are souls trapped in subtle bodies like ghosts, but with a notable difference," explained Mrityaa. "Futuras are beings that die with their mind on plans for the future." "Fixated with the future?" asked Anuradha. "It is the nature of the mind to either wallow in memories or keep making plans for the future. Come to think of it, even people with bodies who live in the past are ghosts."

"And those who live in the future are..." said Anuradha. "Futuras!" chorused the apparitions. "And we want to hear you sing!" said one who rose three feet off the ground and whispered in Anuradha's ears, "Are you entertaining requests, singer?"Anuradha raised an eyebrow. "Anything in particular you have in mind?" she asked. "Can you play us the dead buffalo?" Anuradha shook her head in complete befuddlement. "What about the necrophiliac's ditty? I can help you with the lines," said the Futura.

This appeared to get all the apparitions excited. "Yes! Yes! The Necrophiliac's ditty?" said another one. Our story, it never gets o-old. Restless, me and you so cold. My odes are deep, my love true. Your pale skin, your lips blue.Our beats kill, our songs groove. But why, my love, won't you move? Oh why? Oh why? Oh Why?

Oh why? "Ewwww!" said Anuradha, "How gross is that! I am not singing this song?"

Mrityaa cocked her naughty head and let her thin lips break into a naughty smile. As if one cue, the apparitions began laughing as well. "We have grossed out the woman with the body! What a lovely, lovely day!" She shooed the apparitions away with a wave of her hand. "There is a Gandharva concert tomorrow under the banyan tree. Make sure you do not miss it," said Mrityaa to the apparitions as they began fading out.

When they took to the road, Anuradha wondered aloud about the kinds of bodiless beings on earth. Mrityaa explained that the beings she had seen were not bodiless. They had subtle bodies meant to help them on their onward journey. It was sad that so many of these beings were stuck in the in between, either by choice or because they were trapped. "Who has trapped them?" asked Anuradha. "Why won't they leave?"

"Some are trapped by evil beings who seek power over them. Others are attached to life in the body and fear what the hereafter will bring," explained Mrityaa."Can't the trapped ones be helped?" said Anuradha. "Why don't you and Smashan Kalika help them?" "In the final estimation, none can help another. It is all the cycle of sowing karmic seed and reaping karmic fruit season after season," said Mrityaa. "Very few really want to be helped. These beings are addicted to pain, and they alone have the power to come out of it." The two drove in silence for some time. The car's headlights cut a path through the dense, almost physical darkness surrounding their little world.

Anuradha realized that it had been a while since she had eaten, and it had been a rather light lunch. She decided to stop at the well-known Pundit Dhaba, which served North Indian-style fare. Ramsharan, the owner of the dhaba, noticed the well-dressed woman and little girl walking in. He rushed from his cushioned executive chair, which had a long white hand towel covering much of its headrest to protect it from the perfumed oil in Ramsharan's hair.

Ramsharan Chattopadhyay was tall at 6 feet 3 inches. His straight back, expansive chest, log-like shoulders, and erect posture bore witness to the long hours he had spent in the mud wrestling pit. The child of Bengali Brahmin parents with roots in pre-partition Dhaka, Ramsharan had not married because of his raging obsession with wrestling and devotion to the Hindu deity Hanuman, who prefers that his devotees remain celibate. Ramsharan had been a sickly young child who had been bullied by his taller, stronger Haryanvi classmates. This had spurred him to learn wrestling, which earned him their grudging respect but also made his grades plummet.

His father, Gaurahari Chattopadhyay, a stationmaster with the Indian Railways, tried every trick in the book to get him to focus on academics but failed miserably. At 17, when he failed the eighth grade for the third time, he was thrown out of the family home. Bhavatarini Devi, his mother, had been distraught when this happened, but she could not raise her voice against the patriarch.

CHAPTER THREE

A KARMIC HARVEST

The killer who thinks he slays and his victim who thinks he has been slayed are both ignorant. -Lord Yamaraja in the Katha Upanishad

MRITYAA waved at the old woman standing quietly beside the tandoor. She was staring at Ramsharan with a forlorn expression. "Talk to her," said the man on the Buffalo. "She won't listen to me. Your friend, Yummy, has been waiting forever for her. Like, almost forever." "Who is Yummy?" asked Anuradha. "He refers to himself as Your Friend Yummy. His name is Yamraj, the deity of the crossing to the other realm," explained Mrityaa. "Why won't she move on?" asked Mrityaa. "I cannot move till I apologize to Ramsharan, Amar chhele. My husband gave him such a tough time, and I could not protect him from my husband's anger. The elder one he loved so much, the one who made him so proud with those grades in school and won all those medals, joined his wife in assaulting me when I could not control my motions. I kept pleading with him that it was not something I could control, but they would just not listen. They even abandoned me at the Bhusaval railway station to die. Where was this Yamraj back then?" said Bhavatarini.

"Oh, blame me for everything! I just come when it is time. Mrityaa tells me when it is time. I don't decide this on my own," grumbled Yamraj. "Ask Mrityaa why she did not come earlier." "Oh, come on, Bhavi!" said Mrityaa. "You did have one good son and an excellent daughter-in-law. Was it not all that bleak, was it? They did find you at the station, did they not? They wanted to take you to America, but you would not go."

"Yes," smiled Bhavatarini. "Thank God for my younger son and daughter-in-law. At least, they cared for me in my last days by supporting me financially, but there is only so much that people at an old people's home can do. I missed family. I wished every moment they would take me with them, though. It is not enough to feed, clean, and care for sick old people. I missed my grandchildren. The loneliness made my heart shrivel. They just kept saying it was not possible to stay back. My only regret is that I could not say goodbye to them. Mrityaa just pulled me out of my body before they could fly back from America. Mrityaa, you are a cruel little girl."

Mrityaa responded to the charge with a sheepish expression. Humans are never done with their business! What is a girl to do?" she asked Anuradha. "And," continued Bhavatarini Devi. "This character entered my body and was holding me back in the body while Mrityaa kept pulling me out. It was so painful." The character she was pointing out was a dwarf with a bun on his head, ringed with rudraksha beads, who shrugged at Anuradha as his dog, a ferocious black beauty with resplendent skin and flaming red eyes, licked his hand.

"I am Bhairava. It is my job to clear beings of remnant karma before they leave their existing body, so they can proceed to their next birth with a relatively clean slate. It is a painful process for humans who have not lived their lives to the hilt," he said. "I was not holding her. She just would not let go of the body. I was pushing her out to ease matters and see how I am being repaid for my labors."

Bhavatarini Devi appeared to be taken aback by the outburst. "I am sorry," she smiled sweetly. "Thank you! It does feel very light." Bhairava, who holds the power to liberate souls from the prison of the body so they can ascend to higher realms, mumbled something about the ignorance of human beings. "What?" asked Anuradha. "I was saying, a human being is a seed that holds many forests within its heart. Instead of providing ground for the seed to grow, flower, and bear fruit, people chase security all the time and end up barren, broken, and unfulfilled. It is such unfulfilled beings who have a tough time with death. If you die happy, you drop like a ripe plum!" explained Bhairav.

"Is that directed towards me?" asked Bhavatarini Devi. "You are being personal." "Of course," said the Black Dog. "Every sermon in the world is directed towards you. Why else would nature make you listen to it? Everything is personal." "Shut up! I had a very adventurous life," said Bhavatarini, her eyes widening in surprise. "Did you hear the dog?" "Yeah, he is rude," agreed Anuradha. "No, that is not what I meant," said Bhavatarini. "A talking dog!" "Oh," said Yamraj's buffalo. "You haven't heard me singing yet."

"Is that a threat?" asked Mrityaa mischievously. "Sing us something." The buffalo cleared his throat with a grunt and closed his eyes.

Wrap it up, my sweets,
O Hallo!
Time to leave with the cosmic buffalo.
My skin's shiny, my shanks' lean
Every word I speak, I mean

I fly, my legs I flap
Death Rap!
OH yeah!
It is Death Rap!

Anuradha noted that, suddenly, an audience of a few hundred ghosts and futuras gathered, along with Gandharva musicians who played with ferocious zeal. Anuradha noticed Ramsharan staring at her. All that was visible to him were two strangers. An old woman and her granddaughter are talking, their faces turned in all directions. He had already served them free onion rings, diced radish, lemon slices, and chili. He had been politely waiting for the order.

"Whom are you talking to?" he asked. Mrityaa smiled. "Maa can talk to people who have passed away, and so can I. We are talking to Bhavatarini Devi," she said matter-of-factly. Ramsharan's eyes widened in disbelief. "Who?"

"Your mother. Bhavatarini Devi," repeated Mrityaa. "She died wishing she could tell you how much she missed you all these years. She is sorry that she did not have the courage to stand up to your father." Tears began to flow down Ramsharan's cheeks as his knees buckled beneath him.

It struck Bhavatarini Devi for the first time that Anuradha was in her body and could speak to the living. It got her all excited. "Please tell him that I was waiting for him and his elder brother and my daughter-in-law the day I died.

That I had to die alone in that flat with the two maids, May Thakur ji have mercy on their souls, was proof to me that I was being punished for our abandonment of Ramsharan. I always thought he would return. I had these visions of feeding him kheer sweetened with palm jaggery just the way he liked it, but I did not have the courage to stand up to my husband, and after his passing, I was too dependent on the others to make it possible. Oh, how I hoped he would return and find me." Ramsharan began to sob when Anuradha shared what had been told to her.

"Every day, I prayed to Lord Hanuman to free me from the hatred I felt for my parents. My father's obsession with my grades is a common Bengali thing that I never quite understood, but what was even worse was how my mother never tried to find me. Even after my father died, my brothers did not care to locate me," said Ramsharan. "Today, nothing remains of that time, of those dreams. Tell Mother that I will make some kheer her way and ask her to bless it. I will imagine that she is feeding me, but it won't taste the same without the words of abuse she threw at me and the occasional slap."

Bhavatarini laughed. Yamaraj grinned too. "Hey, everyone is laughing," Mrityaa said, pointing to Bhavatarini. "That is where your mother is standing. If there is anything you would like to tell her, she is listening."

Bhavatarini walked a few steps, raised one ghostly hand, and kept it on her son's shoulders. "How strong he has become, my baby," she said, her voice cracking. "I love you, son. I am very proud of what you have made of your life despite everything."

Ramsharan's eyes began to well again."Maa, you have been the best mother I could have. I pray that I am born again as your son. I wish to lay my head on your lap and smell the detergent and kitchen spices on your cotton sarees again. I will always miss you, Maa." "They appear to be talking to each other," whispered Anuradha. Mother and son were hugging. The heart had found its way.

CHAPTER FOUR

KRISHNA MEETS MRITYAA

Many leave for the abode of Yama every day, and yet people live as if they are immortal. What a wonder! -Yudhishtir in the Mahabharata

Ramsharan tottered back to his chair in a daze, overwhelmed and exhausted, as the servants brought food to Mritya's table. He refused to accept payment for the delicious meal. But an increasing number of apparitions have appeared mid-meal to badger Mrityaa into speaking to Smashan Kalika about letting them have their lives back. "Restore my body," said an old man. "Kalika would never refuse you."

"I won a lottery, and before I could enjoy it, I dropped dead," grumbled another one. "Now, my ungrateful sons are fighting over my money. What a stupid way to go! Give me 48 hours. Just 48 hours!" Hey, Mrityaa! You are not even paying attention," said a stunningly beautiful woman. Wow, what a beauty," said Anuradha. "Are you an actress?" "I am Nia, the zero-size actress," sighed the ghost. "Nobody remembers me anymore. Being dead sucks!" "Regrets. Regrets. Regrets," sighed Mrityaa as they got up to leave.

Ramsharan accompanied Anuradha and Mrityaa to the car. He stood by the road, lost in deep thought as the car sped towards Gurgaon. Nearly 30 minutes passed before Anuradha spoke. "Why do good people like Bhavatarini have to suffer so much? She is such a sweet person," said Anuradha."It is a never-ending journey for a soul flitting from one birth to another. The fruits in one birth cannot be understood on the basis of karma of that birth alone," explained Mrityaa. "One always gets what one deserves."

Anuradha reached home to find her husband, Krishna, in his favorite rocking chair, sipping his evening cup of cinnamon tea. "Hi, sweetheart!" she greeted him with her dimpled smile, which he loved so much. "So, how was your day?" "Regular day, my love," he replied. "Guess whom I met today?" she said. Krishna recognized the look. Anuradha was a sociable person who loved meeting new people. He loved to listen to her recount her exchanges with people she cared about. "Who? Tell me. I am all ears, sweetheart," he said. "I made a new friend, Little Ms. Death," said Anuradha. "She says it is time for me to return home to Lord Krishna." "What?" asked a surprised Krishna."I met a little girl who is death herself in person. I recognize her from my past births. She has been coming to help me discard my old body when it is time for several births now," said Anuradha.

"How can this be true? I have no plans to stay back without you. Where is my ticket to Goloka Vrindavana?" asked Krishna. "I am the ticket," said the voice behind Krishna, who turned back and saw Mrityaa for the first time. "Don't I know you?" asked Krishna. "How did you enter the room?' "I walked in with Amma. You could not see me till she told you about me," explained Mrityaa, her face creasing into a smile.

Anuradha was looking into her husband's eyes. The beautiful brown eyes wore a puzzled look, with a touch of fear and uncertainty. It was unfolding too fast for his comfort, but then he reminded himself that Lord Krishna was their guide and protector on the road ahead. No harm could come to them. Anuradha felt a pang when she realized that this manifestation, this expression of two souls inhabiting two bodies in love with each other, would soon cease to be. She would never see his handsome face once they merged with the Supreme Source.

Krishna fell silent as he attempted to grasp what had just been conveyed to him. He heard. Anuradha spoke as she recounted her adventures earlier that day, beginning, of course, with her meeting with Mrityaa. Krishna rose from his seat and hugged Anuradha. "My darling, this is the beginning of the end," he spoke into her hair. As devotees of Lord Krishna, they had hoped to be in the Lord's arms when life on Earth ended; they had hoped to ascend to a higher plane, way above and beyond the cycle of continuous birth and death, as the ancients called it, moksha.

"Krishna Appa, are you ready?" asked Mrityaa. "So you are home to take us Home?" Krishna smiled. Mrityaa and Anuradha laughed at the weak joke. "Yes," smiled Mrityaa. "Soon. Very soon, Krishna appa."

CHAPTER FIVE

HOLDING ON BY A STRING

No one grants joys or sorrows to us. We merely gather the consequences of our own deeds. -Garuda Purana

"Where are we going next?" asked Anuradha."You already know that. Look at your watch," smiled Mrityaa. It was 10 PM. Karthikeyan! Anuradha remembered that she had promised to stay the night at Curetown, the multi-speciality medical hub in Gurgaon, with her relatives. A distant relative, Karthikeyan, all of 85, was terminally ill. He had expressed the desire to go home.

He had grown tired of the hospital's odors, the uniforms of the medical staff, and the constant whirr of medical machines with their tubes, needles, and wires. Four days ago, he had slipped into a coma. Lata, Karthikeyan's daughter, had told Anuradha tearfully that they would not spare any expense. "He will be fine. This is just a phase," she said, her eyes red and swollen from the tears and the long sleepless nights spent at the hospital.

When Anuradha reached the hospital, she was allowed into the ICU because she was a doctor. A rather comic sight greeted her there. Karthikeyan's astral body was attached to his physical body by the head. He was struggling to free himself, but could not. He was clawing at the life support tubes, but his ghostly hand passed right through them without moving anything. Anuradha was perplexed. "The doctors want to save your life, and you want to leave. You have always been a strong man, Uncle. Put up a good fight," she urged.

Mrityaa had slipped into the ICU effortlessly. She could remain undetected if she wished. "His body has deteriorated to a point where it cannot contain his astral body. He knows that exiting the body completely is the only way of escaping the excruciating pain," explained Mrityaa. "Oh, his body is writhing too," exclaimed Anuradha in horror. "It is sad that Lata has to see her father, her hero, in such a state with all the fight ebbing out of him."Anuradha rushed to Lata, who was sobbing violently. "I am sorry to see you suffer so much. I think you should take him off life support. Let him leave gracefully," advised Anuradha.

Karthikeyan had coronary heart disease along with terminal cancer. Both his kidneys had failed. Yet, the doctors were subjecting his tired, wasted body to expensive, invasive therapies. Mrityaa looked at him sadly and said, "He is in hell". "Is there really such a place?" asked Anuradha."Heavens and hells are not places. They are states of mind, really," said Mrityaa. "A state of elevated happiness is heaven. A state of intense agony is hell."

"So, what is the reason for his hell?' asked Anuradha. "Every action is a seed that holds forests of consequences. Nothing ever goes unrewarded or unpunished," explained Mrityaa. "Karma and consequence chase each other for eternity. Anuradha's attention was drawn to another bed in the ICU. Here, there was another old man in his astral body, weeping piteously. He noticed Mrityaa and walked towards her. "It has been three days and two nights since I died, and the doctors won't break the news to my wife.

She has sold all her gold, spent all our savings, and tomorrow she mortgages our only house. Could you please advise her against taking any more loans? These Doctors will strip her of whatever little she has. How will she live after me?" asked the man. "They are telling her that I am in danger but stable. They know I am dead, but they want to suck the last drop of blood from my wife's body before they let go of the corpse."

Mrityaa laughed as the man became more enraged by the minute. "You do realize why you are suffering, don't you?" Anuradha stared at Mrityaa in incomprehension. "He spent his work life at the government mortuary. The house he is so afraid of losing today has been purchased with the money he extracted from poor folk to have the bodies of their loved ones released. He was pitiless. They had to deal with their loss as well as his heartless demands for money," said Mrityaa. "His wife wore gold bought with that ill-gotten wealth. It is payback time, old man! It is all coming back, is it not?"

Mritya was grinning. He eyes twinkled, and her cheeks dimpled. It was a strangely beautiful sight despite the grim surroundings. The old man stopped his wailing. "Ah, Amma, you know everything," he said. "What should I do now? It is too late to make amends." "Nothing," said Mrityaa. "Leave now. Your wife has her own share of karma and karmic fruits. Hope you remember these lessons in your next birth." The man bowed low. He was at peace.

Anuradha saw the man disappear as he found release.

“If this man and his wife are merely paying for their karmas, are the doctors to blame too?” asked Anuradha. “They are the means through which justice is being served according to the laws of karma, aren’t they?” “Hmmm, responded a man seated on a stool. He was clearly not human. Dressed in purple robes, he was cradling a laptop that appeared to be made of burnished gold.

“Karmic accountancy is a fascinating subject, but you have to give it a few human lifetimes. It kind of grows on you. These souls have been paying and repaying pain to each other over countless lifetimes. I know the number of lifetimes, but I like to say countless because it is my favorite adjective. “And who are you?” asked Anuradha. “He is Chitragupt, the divine accountant,” explained Mrityaa, who turned towards the man. “What’s with the laptop, Chits?” she asked. “It is a must-have accessory to go with my new updated manifestation,” answered Chitragupt.

Anuradha’s curiosity was piqued. “What do you mean by a new updated manifestation?” she asked. Chitragupta twirled the two ends of his rather pointed mustache before answering. “I like to play with names, forms, and appearances when I manifest in time and place. Mrityaa is playing too. She just named me Chits, did she not?” explained Chitragupta. “Don’t you like it?” asked Anuradha. “No. I love it!” laughed Chitragupta. The avalanche of divine beings Anuradha had encountered in the last few hours made her wonder about God. Where was he? Did these deities report to him?

“Am I allowed a question?” asked Anuradha. “Since you are celestial beings and all.” “Fire away!” said Chitragupt. “Ask as many questions as you want." I met Smashan Kalika at the cremation ground, and so many ghosts, futuras, and now you. People offer food, oblations, and incense to all of you. Are you all gods?" asked Anuradha. "Of course. You want me to walk on water or something?" asked Chitragupt. "It is more fun with divine tricks." "But what about the One God?" asked Anuradha, ignoring the off-key Christian reference. "The supreme deity. Are you he... err, it?"

"All numbers, including one, are words in the language of humans. Mathematical language. Numbers are so crude that no divine accountant worth his light would use them for karmic accountancy. All I can say is that the One God is a human fantasy. Many gods are human fantasies, too." "The reality is Many God!" Mirtya announced. "What?" asked Anuradha. "Many God," chorused Chitragupt and Mrityaa.

"God is too many," explained Mrityaa. "And because we are God Stuff, we are too many too." "Do you mean too much?" asked Anuradha. "Yes. God is too much, but God is too many, too," answered Mrityaa. "So, God isn't unity – the one?" asked Anuradha.

"Nope. In this time, place, and space, God is in many forms. In the many beyonds, this time, space and place, God is in many forms in the endless series of the beyonding. None of these forms is limited; they are expressions of the great womb within infinite wombs," said Chitragupt. "But isn't everything with form limited?" asked Anuradha in wonderment.

"Just as this thing and that thing and everything are connected. All forms are informed by items stored in the library of cosmic forms in the divine womb," said Chitragupt. "Where was the pot before the potter shaped it?" "In the mind of the potter," exclaimed Mrityaa.

"And the prototype of the mind of the potter, like all prototypes, is stored in the library of cosmic forms," said Chitragupt. Lata placed her hand on Anuradha's shoulder and looked at her curiously. "Whom are you talking to?" she asked. Mrityaa held Anuradha's hand. Touched by the gesture, Anuradha could not hold back her tears. Uncle is in intense agony. He says he wants to leave now.

These machines are making it very difficult for him. "What is this nonsense?" retorted Lata. "You want me to kill my father by putting him off life support," sobbed Lata. "No, he is ready to move on. I can talk to him," said Anuradha. Karthikeyan's attention was drawn to the conversation.

He stopped struggling with his body. "I want her to take me home to my grandchildren. Put my bed by the window so I can see the gulmohur. I want to leave with all my little sweethearts around me," he said. "I had asked her not to bring me to the hospital, but she refused to heed my requests."

Anuradha cupped Lata's face in her palm and told her that Karthikeyan wanted to return home to his grandchildren. Lata was stunned as Anuradha was repeating words that her father had spoken to her before he slipped away. She walked to her father's bed and took his frail hand in hers. "I know you can hear me. It breaks my heart to let you go, but I will do it if that is what you would like to do," she said. This agitated Karthikeyan. "Tell the fool to get on with it. This girl has always been wood-headed. I cannot tell you how much of a struggle this is."

Two hours later, Lata asked the hospital to take Karthikeyan off support. He felt very weak inside his ravaged body. An hour later, he was home surrounded by friends, family, and the grandchildren he loved to bits. It was warm outside but breezy. Karthikeyan felt the warm breeze graze his cheek as a crow cackled on the Gulmohur in bloom outside.

Anuradha watched Karthikeyan's subtle body disengage from his physical self. He stood outside the confines of his old prison for a while as everyone around him wept. He was at peace. Finally. His attachments severed, he looked at Mrityaa for a moment, smiled, and faded into the ether. Outside, in the broad air-conditioned corridors of the hospital, Anuradha's eyes met with Yamraja astride on his black buffalo. He smiled as he waved at Mrityaa and Anuradha.

CHAPTER SIX

SHYAMOLEE'S STORY

Once, as I was burying one of my dead selves, the grave-digger came by and said to me, "Of all those who come here to bury, you alone I like." Said I, "You please me exceedingly, but why do you like me?" "Because," said he, "They come weeping and go weeping, you only come laughing and go laughing." -Kahlil Gibran in The Grave Digger

The day dawned bright and sunny. As she did every day, Anuradha woke up with the Lord's name, chanting the Mahamantra, "Hare Krishna, Hare Krishna, Krishna Krishna, Hare Hare, Hare Ram, Hare Ram, Ram Ram Hare Hare." She finished her morning chores and meditation and was ready for her day in a lovely cotton sari. As she was contemplating how to manifest Mrityaa's presence, Mrityaa suddenly appeared. Mrityaa was always with her, becoming visible whenever she thought of her. Anuradha found it miraculous and enchanting.

"We are going to meet Mrs. Shyamolee Das today", said Mrityaa. Anuradha brightened up instantly on hearing the old Bengali lady's name. Mrs. Shyamolee Das was her patient and lived nearby. Anuradha was very fond of her because she reminded Anuradha of her Meena Patti. Fair, chubby with a ready smile, Mrs Shyamolee was a hypertensive patient.

Anuradha made home visits to monitor her blood pressure. Abeer Das was her only son, and he was very considerate towards his mother. The lady had a nice daughter-in-law and grandson, too. Anuradha loved her visits to their home because everyone was cheerful and it was lovely and friendly. They would have a typical family physician visit with her and discuss all their common topics. Abeer had kept Anuradha informed about the failing condition of Shyamolee's kidneys.

They had consulted a Renal specialist who had told Abeer that her kidneys were in chronic renal failure and would stop working in a few years' time. There were options for her treatment like dialysis, but Abeer had refused to let his Mother undergo such complicated and invasive treatment. Anuradha was very happy with his wisdom and consideration for his Mother.

And now it was time for Shyamolee to go Home to her husband and Krishna. She would actually be a peaceful person even after she left this world. Anuradha was confident about that. Anuradha made idlis and sambar for her husband's breakfast and then woke him up. Her husband was happy to see her in such good cheer. She told him about Mrs. Shamolee, and they both shared the simple breakfast followed by a cup of their favorite cinnamon tea.

Anuradha bid Krishna goodbye and set off on her mission, hand in hand with Mrityaa, who had refused the delicious breakfast with a dimpled smile. "I don't eat, Amma," smiled Mrityaa, who probably ate people for breakfast, thought Anuradha, amused by her own surmises. They walked to the door of Abeer Das's flat, and Mrityaa disappeared, leaving Anuradha to compose herself before meeting her sweet patient.

Abeer had called her in the morning for a regular check-up; little did he know that it would be his Mother's last check-up. Anuradha greeted the maid warmly and was led to Shyamolee's room. The old lady looked frail and tired today, but she was smiling cheerfully as always. Anuradha sat beside her and took her hand, gently reassuring her with her smile.

They had a regular meeting, and Anuradha did not mention anything to Shyamolee or Abeer, who came to see her shortly after. Somehow, Shyamolee sensed that something was different today and started talking to Anuradha about her husband, Neelkanth. She told Anuradha about his wonderful sense of humour and his kind ways. She remembered him fondly and asked Anuradha if he would be waiting for her on the other side when she passed on. Anuradha reassured her with an affirmation, and Shyamolee was happy.

She squeezed Anuradha's hand and mumbled her thanks through teary eyes. " You are such a beautiful soul," she told Anuradha, kissing her forehead. Anuradha felt blessed and was teary-eyed herself. Abeer offered her a cup of tea, which she declined, and then she left their home, knowing she would be called the next day to make the death certificate, as Anuradha was their family physician. She really admired Abeer for allowing his Mother the luxury of being at home, among family and friends, while she breathed her last.

Life is beautiful, thought Anuradha, and while she walked home, there she was, Mrityaa, back with her. "How did I do?" she asked Mrityaa, who rolled her eyes heavenwards in admiration. "You are too kind, Anu Amma," she said, giving her a hug. Anuradha headed home. She felt a bit tired and took a nap. She dreamed of Shyamolee, seeing her surrounded by both her current family and all her relatives who had passed before her. Shyamolee looked peaceful and serene. Thank God for His mercies.

CHAPTER SEVEN

YAMRAJ'S POINT

Have no doubt! All kings, O son, are destined to experience hell. Dharma to Yudhishtir in the Mahabharata

Mrityaa rushed out of the ICU and stood before Yamraj. "Hey!" she said. "Has it been a long shift for you?" "Yeah," said Yamraj. "You have kept me busy. People are dying by the dozens since you have an assistant to help you out." He winked at Anuradha so she understood the joke. "Now that we are friends, may I ask you where it is that you take these souls?" Anuradha asked Yamraj.

"To the place of the great forgetting and the next leap," explained Yamraj. "The great forgetting is the place where all memories of the present life are pushed into the unconscious. After that is done, the soul's karmic bank begins looking for an appropriately challenging womb to be born in. Without challenges, there is no growth, and without growth, there is no great leap." "What about the great leap? What does it mean?" asked Anuradha. "It is the point where the soul descends from the higher planes to earth, the land of return," responded Yamraj.

"Why is it called the land of return?" asked Anuradha. "One has to be born on earth and as a human to return to the Great Source, the Many God," explained Yamraj. Even the celestials who long to play with the Many God crave a human birth." "Does God play?" asked Anuradha. Of course," Mrityaa piped in. "We are all the playmates of the Many God." Chitragupt joined the group, his gold laptop tucked under his arm.

"The Source," said Chitragupt with a faraway look in his eyes. "It is where everything is emerging and merging in waves. The Source is a place of peace and tranquility, unlike the Earth, which is a gym with a very punishing schedule. The suffering is for a purpose, but humans in their ignorance do not wish to leave for the higher planes when it is time to leave. They celebrate the birth of a child but fear Mrityaa, who ends earthly suffering and clears the way for their return to the source, the Many God. Humans cry when someone dies after leading a full life because they are selfish. They are mostly thinking about themselves. They are worrying about their own survival. How foolish!"

Mrityaa tilted her head curiously and scrunched her face into a scowl. "Amma, he is right, but it is not as serious as he makes it to be. Accountants have a talent for making things appear serious," she said. "It is all the play of the Many God, and we are all his little playmates.""Will play with me, the Many God. Does he love me?" asked a sweet voice. "Mom says Krishna loves me."

Everyone turned in the direction of the sound. It was a little girl of about seven years old, clutching a pink stuffed teddy. She had lost all her hair, including that on her eyebrows. Despite her frail frame, bony shoulders, and reed-thin arms, she was a beautiful child with her huge eyes that shone like black pools of light from her fat baby face.

“I am sure he loves you to bits,” said Yamraj. “I often visit Vaikuntha Goloka, the eternal abode of Lord Krishna. He throws great parties.” “Yes,” said Paundraka, Yamraj’s buffalo dreamily. “The grass is really greener in Goloka. The cows have it really good there.” Anuradha’s eyes began to tear up. “Is Krishna the Many God?” she asked haltingly.

“Indeed. Krishna is the favourite personhood of the Many God. As we grow higher senses and experience him at one level, he beckons us to ascend to an even higher level. At every level, we get even higher senses. The eyes grow more and more divine, and the Personhoods of the Many God keep unfolding before us. Neither the seeking nor the finding ends in this love story,” explained Chitragupt. “As we keep seeking intimacy, he reveals an even deeper side that we have not yet touched or experienced. This unfolding of the lover and the beloved is the business of the universe.”

The little girl could not make head or tail of the explanation. “Huh?” is all she could say. “The accountant is saying Krishna is awesome,” said Mrityaa. “You are going to have a great time in Goloka.” “Come on, hop on board, said Paundraka. “We have a long way to go.” The little girl, Piu, was not sure. Her mother was in the hospital room a few meters away. She had to leave the body suddenly.

Cancer had ravaged her entire body. Little Piu had tried very hard to console her mother. She had stood in her astral form in the room, which was haunted by the sad ghost of another child, a boy of twelve who was waiting for his father to return. Ronak had been abandoned to the mercy of the hospital. The bills had been paid, and the best care had been provided. Ronak had lost his mother as a child, and his father had little time to spare from his carpet business spread across three continents.

So, he had passed away, his eyes glued to the entrance of the room in the pediatric wing of Cure town. Anuradha beckoned Piu closer. "Is something bothering you?" she asked Piu as she kept a hand gently on Piu's shoulder. "Yes, you are the only person with a body who can see me. Could you please tell my mom that I am fine?" asked Piu. "Tell her I am not in pain anymore and that I love her. I am going to meet Krishna, the Many-God, in Goloka Vrindavana. I will be waiting for her and Papa."

"What is your mother's name?" asked Anuradha. Piu answered both questions in the affirmative. "Is your father here too?" Anuradha asked. "Yes, the entire family is here," said Piu. Yamraj turned Paundraka around.

The group heard painful wails as they approached the room. Everyone in Pia's little world was present in the room. Her grandparents, her parents, and her uncle and aunt, along with the extended family members who had supported Pia's parents as they battled her cancerous brain tumor. Her engineer father and artist mother were very much in love. They had everything one could ask for. The family had a beautiful home and several cars. They had an active social life filled with parties, holidays, and several luxuries.

Life was perfect except that the couple did not have a child after seven years of marriage despite prayers and repeated visits to the best specialists around. Then one day, Priya discovered that she was pregnant. The couple was ecstatic.

Who could have predicted that the seven years of laughter, naughty antics, and joy-filled milestones in Pia's life would end here, like this? The Naths dedicated themselves to treating everything they had, but Piu, their Piu, could not be saved. Priya was struck by the unfairness of life.

As the ghostly entourage entered the room, Anuradha's eyes fell on Ronak's face. His face lit up before turning darker. His shoulders slumped, and he sat at the foot of his old bed, which was one of two such beds in the room. Anuradha's heart sank when she noticed his great sadness. It was deeper and more unsettling than the sight of Pia's mother cradling her daughter's wilted body in her arms. "Piu is here standing beside me," announced Anuradha. "She is fine and ready to leave for the higher planes."

The family stared at Anuradha, too shocked for words. Priya hugged Piu even harder and kissed her collarbone as the tears flowed even more copiously. Her husband stood up and spoke. "I don't know who you are and how you know about Pia. Please leave us alone. We are grieving for our child," he said. Piu was visibly distressed. "Papa, no more strawberry ice creams at The Three Joys store," she said. "Mommy, don't weep. I am going to meet Krishna."

Anuradha began to repeat every word Piu spoke. Soon, everyone in the room believed that Piu was indeed there. "We are sorry we could not save you," sobbed Priya. "You tried Mommy but it was time to leave. I was in so much pain but I feel so light now. I am peaceful now," said Piu. "How will you manage without me?" asked Priya.

"I have already made new friends on the other side. I feel safe and protected. Please do not worry any more. It makes me sad," said Piu as she smiled at little Roshan who was quietly looking at the drama being enacted before his eyes. "Won't you come with me?" asked Piu. "He will because today is his big day. His father should be coming to the ward in a few minutes. I found his number and called him to the ward," smiled Anuradha.

Piu walked towards her parents and gave her mother a kiss and hugged her father. Her mother sensed a familiar warmth envelop her. She could smell Piu. Confused, Priya looked at Anuradha. "She is hugging you two," said Anuradha.Roshan walked up to Anuradha. The celestials were smiling reassuringly at him. Roshan threw a friendly arm around Paundrika's neck and hugged him. "If I meet my father today, I have no reason to keep hanging here. I will leave. Maybe, he will join me in the higher spheres."

"Ah, no!" exclaimed Chitragupt. "You are destined to be born his son again very soon. It says in my records that you will be reunited with your father." "Wow, can you arrange that?" asked Anuradha. Mrityaa shook her head. "No, he does not. Your karmas are taking you in that direction and that appears to be your last thought. Your father has already met your new mother. It is just that he does not know that he will marry her and have you," she said.

Roshan's father Abhimanyu Jain walked into the room with a big box of chocolates, toys and some new clothes. "Where is my son," he asked everyone in the room. "He is right by your side and all smiles," said Anuradha. "He is asking why you did not get the red balloons like you do on every visit?" "Because I have carried him home," laughed Yamraj. "He is not taking birth anytime soon."

Abhimanyu bent on his knees. Roshan threw his arms around his father and hugged him with his phantom arms. "Good bye," said Piu! Good bye" repeated Roshan. The celestials began to fade along with the two children. There was a ball of light, which enveloped them and then turned into a tunnel that led to the sky. They rose higher and higher till the tunnel closed. The ball then exploded into a happy bright pink that washed everything in the room.

CHAPTER EIGHT

THE MATRICES OF MANY TENTACLED METAPHORS

All men are bound by fate and personal effort. These two forces are all that are. There is nothing else. -Krpacharya in the Mahabharata

Paundrika trotted out of the room with Yamraj on his back. Anuradha and Mrityaa followed them out, as did Chitragupta. Anuradha saw a bearded Muslim turning beads with his eyes closed. He was rocking back and forth as he did the rounds mumbling phrases from his holy book. "How have you been?" the Muslim asked Yamraj."Good. What about you?" asked Yamraj? "I see that you are getting ready to leave this plane."

Anuradha stared in amazement. Not only did this living person see Yamraj, he was addressing a Hindu divinity that was a mythical character for her before she met Mrityaa. Mrityaa cocked her head and looked at Anuradha. "His time is near. I will be visiting him soon. Being an awakened one, he knows who we are," she explained. She found the idea of Hindu divinities servicing

Muslims hilarious. "So, it is Yamraj who collects the souls of the Inuit, the French and the Africans too. It must be very confusing for them to see Indians in funny costumes. They must wonder at how they have wasted their lives believing in the wrong God!" laughed Anuradha.

Paundrika turned back to look Anuradha in the eye and raised one sad eyebrow. "We are beings from the higher realms. You can only see us in the mirror of your personal metaphor, which is but one mirror in the splendorous matrices of the many tentacled metaphor," said Paundrika. "The Muslim sees us differently as he has a different mirror in his head." "So, you are merely a metaphor and this is some sort of dream?" asked Anuradha.

"Everything is a metaphor for something else and every reality is a dream in a sleep of many layers. Every time you wake up, you are waking up in another dream, which will break eventually in a higher dream," explained Mrityaa. "All you are seeing is real till you wake up in a higher level." "Indeed," said Chitragupt. "The sandwich of dream has many layers. The sleeps are loafs and every level of reality is a level of filling." The metaphor of the sandwich made Anuradha hungry. The celestials took leave of Mrityaa and Anuradha as the two headed to the lavishly done cafeteria of Cure town, which had a menu that had twenty pages with 30 items on each page.

In one corner of a cafeteria, his head bowed, sat a ghost – a young man – who noticed Mrityaa. "You had to come just before I could experience the happiest day of my life!" he said bitterly. "Could you not wait?" Mrityaa cocked her head on one side and smiled sweetly. This was a question she was asked often. "I have already told you Mani that I do not decide anything. I come when your karmas ripen. You should just quit this plane. Leave!" said Mrityaa. "I was telling Maa that humans are never done with their business. Most humans keep clinging to the body." Mani noticed Anuradha looking at him. "Hey, you can see me! What magic is this? It is scary!" he laughed nervously.

"I have been asking Mrityaa to write a letter to my love and she says she is not allowed to do it. She paid me a visit a day before my wedding and I had no chance to say goodbye."Mrityaa and Anuradha sat across the dining table facing Mani. "Hey, Mani!" said Mrityaa. "Why do you think I got Amma here?" Mani's ghostly eyes brimmed with tears. "Maa, could you please help me? I will make it very short.""Sure. No problem at all," smiled Anuradha as she rummaged her purse for her notebook and pen.

Mani clasped both his hands as he rested them flat on the stainless steel dining table and closed his eyes to shut out any distractions. He then craned his neck till he appeared to be looking at the ceiling. Anuradha took her phone out and began to type:

Dear Amba,

It happened too suddenly! Here, in the in-between, as I linger on with a body that is lighter than light and subtler than thought, I hang by the thinnest skein of matter to this plane of existence and to you my beloved, my sweet. I encircle you helplessly as you grieve my sudden passing and sometimes you sense that I am around. I miss you. I miss us. I miss the certainty of your presence in a changing world. I miss the music of your breath, the throb of your heart, the meanderings of your impulsive mind. What remains now for me except for memories of beautiful days and nights spangled with a million stars? I grieve for you and for those I have left behind even as you grieve for me. I will not ask you to get over me because how can one ever get over the passing of a loved one? Even when you find another lover and love him deeply, Life is short but love is forever. I want you to know that I am not gone. I shall blow you a kiss after you read this letter and I will expect you to give me the smile I love so much before I leave.

Always in your heart. Love, Mani.

Anuradha's eyes filled with tears as she wrote. Mrityaa sighed! An hour later, Anuradha spied Mani sprawled on the family sofa as Amba opened the door. He acknowledged her with a gentle nod of the head as they explained their mission. Amba's swollen eyes rested on Anuradha's face as she stared in stupefaction at what had just been told to her.

Desperate, like a drowning person clutching at a straw, Amba urged Anuradha to read the letter, and as the words tumbled out, fresh tears filled the brown pools of her eyes. They poured in great sadness. "Is he here?" asked Amba who recognized Mani in the letter. "Can he see me?"

Mani sat upright on the sofa as Anuradha pointed toward him. "I love you, Mani!" said Amba as she stood before him. "I love you too, Amba," answered Mani as he returned her smile. "I am gone but not dead. We shall meet again." Amba looked at Anuradha and almost repeated Mani's words. "If death is not the end, I shall meet my Mani in another place, another lifetime but it is going to be very sad without him." Mani bowed low first to Mrityaa and then to Anuradha as his body began to turn into a bright disc of light, which then disappeared in a flash. Mani had ascended to a higher plane.

CHAPTER NINE

RADHIKA COMES HOME

Ek Omkar Satnam .He is One. He is Omkar, the Supreme Truth. He is the creator, beyond fear, beyond hatred. He is the timeless form. Never born, self-creating .He is attained by the Guru's Grace. - Guru Nank Dev

Radhika was very close to Anuradha from their Medical college days. Both of them became friendly very early in their college life because both were fond of singing and would be together practicing for their Annual festivals. They even attended Youth festivals in other colleges when they had to travel together by train and so they became inseparable friends, attending all classes together and even visiting the college canteen together for tea breaks.

Life separated them for twenty years after college and as luck would have it, they met again when Radhika moved to Anuradha's city and they discovered each other on Facebook. Soon they exchanged addresses and planned a visit. Both were very excited about meeting each other after so long. They had learnt from their phone conversations about each other.

Anuradha had been married and was blessed with two sons and a daughter, whereas, Radhika was still single. They met and were tearful when they gave each other a hug. But soon they were roaring with laughter thinking about their college days and all the fun they had together. To their joy, they discovered that both of them had turned spiritual, were reading the Bhagvad Gita and were also a lot into alternative therapies, Yoga and meditation.

Radhika was a general physician and Anuradha taught Physiology and both had a lot of common experiences as healers. To their delight, they discovered that both believed in the natural healing techniques and did not rely too much on modern medicines. God had made them happy by helping each other with their long lost friendship. Both were overjoyed and marveled at Krishna's Grace and Blessings.

It was only after a few meetings, they were determined to keep in touch now, that Anuradha noticed that Radhika was not her usual cheerful self. She had a lot of sadness in her eyes and whenever Anuradha asked her about why she chose to remain single, she avoided the topic and gave some lame excuse. This time however Anuradha was determined to know the truth about her friend.

She asked her point blank and Radhika was grateful for that because she too wanted to unburden herself. Radhika told Anuradha about how she had fallen in love with a colleague in a hospital she worked after her internship. They both were pursuing General Medicine and were doing their post-graduation. Radhika's eyes lit up with those beautiful memories.

She recalled how she had met Rohan and how they had instantly connected and became very good friends. Being post-graduate students together is a very close association and Anuradha knew that.

They had been together day in day out and had studied together eaten together and become the best of friends, Radhika told her. With time their friendship had become a relationship of the heart and by the time they finished their Post-graduation, they had decided to get married. Even though they belonged to different castes and communities and spoke different languages, they had been too much in love to even think about those differences. Both sets of parents had agreed to their match.

Two days before their wedding, Rohan had gone out with his friends on his bike for a party and on his return late at night, he met with an accident. A truck collided with him and unfortunately, Rohan lost his life. Radhika came to know about it the next morning and was totally devastated. She did not know what to do with her life. She could not imagine living even a single day without Rohan and even talking about it with Anuradha made Radhika cry inconsolably. It was now that Anuradha understood the reason for her friend's sadness.

She kept talking to Radhika for a long time that night. Both of them were spending the night at Radhika's apartment. They did not sleep till the wee hours of the morning and by the time dawn was breaking, they were exhausted but they were both happy that they had shared Radhika's grief and her burdens definitely were lighter.

Anuradha told Radhika to get counseling for her grief and they also discussed various shlokas from the Bahgvad Gita and the other spiritual books that both had read. Radhika understood everything theoretically but she just could not cope with her loss. She kept looking for the same person she had lost, in other people she met after that, and she could never find Rohan, which is not a mystery because God makes each individual unique.

And each relationship unique too. Anuradha wisely told her to keep an open mind when she met new people and that would probably help her to love again. It had been seventeen years since Rohan had passed on. And Radhika had not found love again. Radhika's old Mother lived with her and was happy and grateful for Anuradha's support and love. The next few days were joyful for them all because Anuradha spent a lot of time with Radhika. Coaxing her to start singing again, watching movies with her and reliving all their college memories. They went shopping together and also attended some music concerts and workshops on Spirituality.

They would also have a lot of serious discussions sometimes. Anuradha shared all that she knew and had learnt in her spiritual learning with Radhika, urging her to ask questions whenever she had any. The second chapter in the Bhagvad Gita was a favorite with Anuradha who quoted the shlokas verbatim for Radhika and patiently explained to her that the Soul is immortal and does not pass on when the body dies. The body is made of the five elements and when the soul leaves the body the elements are dissolved in Nature.

Without the Soul, the body is useless. The soul discards bodies like worn off garments and takes new bodies to fulfill the desires of the heart which get stored in the Soul as sanskars and are carried to the next birth. The person who dies has not really gone anywhere, he in only not visible to the five senses of his relatives who survive, since his body is gone. The individual soul (the Jivatman) merges with the Universal Soul (The Paramatman) after the body dies. The Paramatman is Krishna and is full of light and unconditional Love. So the individual soul is actually in a lot of bliss after merging with the Paramatman (The Universal Self, Brahman, The Reality or Consciouness) so there is no reason for us to grieve.

When we lose our loved ones. We should be happy for them and rejoice for they have reached Home to our beloved Father. "Aren't you happy to reach Home, Radhika?" asked Anuradha, to lighten up the conversation and Radhika laughed loud, "and how happy your Mother is to see you", she continued and both Mother and daughter exchanged a grateful look for the excellent example that Anuradha had given.

Anuradha also explained to Radhika, from her knowledge of other books on NDE's (Near Death Experiences) that she had read, that people who died and reached the Source, but decided to come back to Earth to be with their beloved ones here, had related stories of experiencing a beautiful unconditional love and a Light so bright that they were rejuvenate by It.

They could see that we are not weak human beings locked up in our puny bodies but we are energy fields with unlimited possibilities and we can actually achieve anything that we wish to do on this Earth plane. If only we knew our Power and lived our life happily and joyfully, we could manifest almost anything. Radhika felt happy and rejuvenated with her conversations with Anuradha and longed to achieve her dreams and lead a beautiful, happy life.

All these events had transpired within a span of about a year since they had connected again and it was a very beautiful time for all of them. Unfortunately, Anuradha had to leave town to attend to her ailing Aunt and had not been able to continue her association with Radhika. She had assumed though, that Radhika would find her own way and be happy forever.

When Anuradha returned after a long span of six months, she met Radhika one evening, hoping to have a lot of fun with her. She met her at a Mall and was appalled to see that Radhika looked weak and tired and even more sad than she had been before. On enquiring, she came to know that Radhika had tried to start a new relationship with someone, after Anuradha had gone. Within a few weeks she had found someone, only to be disappointed once again when she discovered accidently that the person was already married and was only looking for some excitement. Radhika was broken and had decided to withdraw into her shell again.

Anuradha was too overwhelmed with her story and decided to leave her friend to heal herself at the pace that she found comfortable. Anuradha left her friend with the promise that she was always available and would be with her whenever she wanted.Anuradha felt a bit sad and helpless that she had not been able to help her friend, but she left it all to Krishna as she knew that only He could solve such difficult problems. She often prayed for her friend and went on with her life, always keeping Radhika in her prayers.

The next day of Mrityaa's mission found Anuradha bright and cheerful, ready to take on the world. She finished her morning chores, took a shower, meditated on her Lord Krishna and lit the lamp, singing Om Jai Jagdish Hare, as was her daily practice. After making Poha for breakfast, she woke up her husband and they had their breakfast in silence, the same question on both their minds, who would it be today?

Mrityaa appeared as always and looked amused to see them both so serious. She decided to play a prank on them and hid herself behind the fridge. "Find me, Anu Maa", she called and it took only a second for Anuradha to find her and give her a warm hug. Both were joyous to be with each other. "Radhika it is', said Mrityaa matter-of-factly, and both Anuradha and Krishna groaned, "Ohhhhhhhh NO!!!!" they exclaimed together. Anuradha had shared Radhika's story with Krishna at that time when she had been in touch with her and Krishna had applauded her for the wonderful support and love she was showering on Radhika.

After they parted too Anuradha had shared her disappointment with Krishna, and he had encouraged her saying that she had done the right thing by leaving it all to The Lord. Both of them had sincerely prayed to Krishna for Radhika and today, they heard her name after a good three decades. Anuradha immediately felt guilty for not reaching out to her friend earlier, but she knew in her heart that many times she had called Radhika in those early days and had not received a favourable response from her, because Radhika was too much into her shell. After a while she had given up, and left it all to Krishna, as was her practice with any difficult problem. She did pray for Radhika very often but did not know that she was on her death bed.

Mrityaa told them that Radhika had been suffering from Cancer of the Uterus and had undergone surgery and Radiation to heal herself. The treatment had worked for some time, but the cancer had already spread to her lungs and so she was in therapy again. Radhika's rich Uncle had supported her financially after her Mother had passed on. Now Radhika was admitted in a hospice which was specialized in care for the terminally ill patients. She was very comfortable materially, but her spirit had broken and she really needed healing before she passed on, otherwise she would carry all those negative sanskars to her next birth too.

Anuradha set off with Mrityaa with determination in her heart. She told Krishna that she would make up for all the years that she had lost being away from her friend. She would be spending the maximum time available to her with her friend so he should be prepared for that. It was still not too late, Anuradha realized with gratitude to the Lord for giving her this opportunity. Mrityaa led Anuradha to the hospice where Radhika was staying. "How do you know all the places?", she asked Mrityaa with amazement. "I am all places, remember Anu Maa", said Mrityaa with her dimpled smile.

Mrityaa left Anuradha at the hospice reception and disappeared. Anuradha enquired about the room where Radhika was staying and went to see her immediately. She knocked on the room door and it was opened by an elderly gentleman, she assumed must be Radhika's Uncle. She introduced herself and walked upto Radhika's bed. She was sad to see that Radhika was in a very bad state, totally shrunk, in pain and had aged considerably. Anuradha on the other hand was glowing radiantly and even more beautiful than in her youth, the light of consciousness shining from within. She gave Radhika a warm hug and asked her why she hadn't reached out to her friend earlier. Radhika broke down and sobbed uncontrollably.

She couldn't let go of Anuradha and couldn't even speak, she was in so much agony and pain. After some time, she started coming out of her disturbed state of mind and could speak a few words. She requested her Uncle to leave them alone for a while, so that she could speak to Anuradha and share her heart's pain.

"I would have perished if it hadn't been for Krishna and His Love", said Anuradha to Radhika. She told her friend that once we are on this spiritual journey, we should never look back and fall back into our earlier, faulty ways because those will always lead us away from the Lord and life would be difficult and so stressful. As we progress in this path, the Lord shows us that He is the Only Reality and all else that we experience here on Earth is only his illusion (Maya).

"So, is this an illusion, what we are talking now?", asked Radhika and Anuradha said, "yes". Anuradha revealed to Radhika, this secret of the Bhagvad Gita, which one comes to know by repeated and disciplined reading of this sacred scripture. "We are all in a dream world, we are only playing a role in this dream world". She asked Radhika, "Would you take your dream seriously?" and Radhika said , "no". "Only
Consciousness exists, only Krishna is Real, all else is a dream and we are caught up in the dream because we forget the Reality".

"Krishna gives us troubles to remind us that we have forgotten him. When we remember Him, then He slowly takes us back to the Reality by giving us different messages and repeatedly gives us this knowledge and lures us back to Him". "And when we come back to

Him, He is the happiest because we have reached Home to Him". "And we are delivered from this world of dreams, this world of births and deaths forever."

"Do you think I could go back to Krishna, when I pass on?" asked a tearful Radhika and Anuradha reassured her, "Of course my darling, you are going back to Krishna, that is for sure". "You could stay with Him forever if you so desire", said Anuradha and Radhika was happy at last.

She could see that she has been really foolish by being away from spirituality and by allowing the world's temporary troubles to overwhelm her and to make her doubt Krishna's Love. Now she felt contented and relaxed. She understood that only Krishna is the Reality, only Consciousness and no duality. Our life here on Earth is a mirage. We are running towards temporary pleasures, and we forget the most important aspects of spirituality, which will give us bliss and happiness which is ever-lasting. At last Radhika was at peace.

She felt really grateful to Anuradha for her timely help and support. She was ready to go to Krishna with complete surrender. Anuradha was overjoyed that her mission was a success. She had given Radhika the best gift of her life. The two friends hugged each other warmly and exchange a tearful farewell. Anuradha was happy and returned home with relief and gratitude to her beloved Lord Krishna. She knows that whenever Radhika passes on, she would be happy and peaceful.

Mrityaa was home before her and was talking to her husband. Both of them were waiting for her with a large cup of tea and biscuits to welcome her. And she was so happy to be home after a difficult but fruitful day. They all realize that it is never too late, a person can go home to the Lord, whenever they feel like. It is only His grace and blessings which are needed.

CHAPTER TEN

HEMLATA LOSES HER BELOVED FATHER

Whenever an experience comes to an end, a gathering of friends, a vacation, your children leaving home, you die a little death. If you can learn to accept and even welcome the endings in your life, you may find that the feeling of emptiness that initially felt uncomfortable turns into a sense of inner spaciousness that is deeply peaceful. By learning to die daily in this way; you open yourself to Life.- Eckhart Tolle in Stillness Speaks

Hemlata loved her father a lot and was deeply attached to him. Her father was her whole world and she depended on him for everything. She believed that her father would always be with her. The thought of losing him forever did not enter her mind and even if it did, she would ignore it.

Hemlata had lost her Mother when she was three years old and knew only one parent, her Father, he was both Mother and Father to her. He brought her up with the utmost love and care. The happy years passed quickly and Hemlata grew up to be a beautiful young lady. She was confident and strong. She started working and supporting her father who was old by now and had retired from his job.

As time passed, Hemlata's father became old and frail. He wanted to be there for his little girl and protect her from all the evil in the world. But his health kept deteriorating with time. He was a diabetic for 30 years and though he was highly disciplined in his eating habits, the disease was destroying all his organ systems slowly and steadily. He was feeling increasingly breathless and his daughter called Anuradha to see him. They lived in the same society for years and Anuradha knew them well.

Mrityaa had already told Anuradha that Hemlata's Father was terminally ill and could not be saved, but Anuradha would have to deal with this case very carefully as Hemlata was very deeply attached to her beloved Father and had nobody in her life except him. She had not even found a life-partner because she was so close to her Father that she did not want another person to be in their life and take her away from her Father.

Anuradha met the duo and after examining Hemlata's Father, she sent them to a nearby multi-speciality Hospital as the elderly gentleman was suffering from a lot of complicated conditions and would require immediate hospitalization. In the Hospital, Hemlata's Father was examined by many Doctors and they came to the conclusion that he had a serious heart disease, with many of his coronary arteries being blocked.

He first had to undergo angiography, the injection of a dye into his coronary arteries and radiography. He was diagnosed to be suffering from coronary heart disease of an advanced level. He needed surgery immediately, the Doctors advised. They admitted him to the hospital and started treatment. From day one, the hospital was a dreadful ordeal for the poor old man.

He was put on an intravenous line and medicines were continually pumped into him. His legs had developed swelling and the skin had severe cellulitis. The Doctors kept giving the strongest antibiotics to deal with the infection. His kidneys which were already damaged due to the effect of his diabetes, started to fail, due to the side effect of the antibiotics. He was put on dialysis. His veins were punctured on both sides of the neck and the dialysis had its own disastrous side effects.

The poor gentleman's health started deteriorating. All he wanted was to go home and die peacefully in his home environment. But it was impossible to take him home in this condition. Hemlata felt she was in the worst horror story of her life. All her life's savings were spent on the huge hospital bills and she had not been able to buy even a moment's painless existence for her father. She eventually lost him and that made her completely shattered.

Despite his deteriorating health, the girl was hoping against hope that God would work a miracle and her father's life would be saved. She felt betrayed and devastated when he could not survive. Her heart was torn into pieces because her beloved father had suffered so much. She felt helpless and angry with the whole Universe and her grief was uncontrollable when she went to see him getting cremated. How she longed for his reassuring smile and his strong arms around her. Why was life never fair to her? He had been the only one in her life and now she would be all alone forever.

Anuradha met Hemlata, after the cremation was over and she had come home, to an empty life. Anuradha spoke to Hemlata, trying to console her and explain to her God's great design and how Death was an inevitable part of every human being's life. She kept talking to Hemlata for many hours but the girl did not respond to Anuradha at all and kept crying inconsolably. Anuradha had no option but to leave Hemlata alone and return home to her husband.

Before going home, Anuradha kept a beautiful picture of Radha Krishna which she had got from the nearby temple, and a copy of the Bhagwad Gita in Hemlata's house and left. To her surprise and delight, when Anuradha went to meet Hemlata the next day, she saw her looking marginally better. She had stopped crying and was trying to read the Bhagwad Gita.

This gave Anuradha an opportunity to speak to Hemlata about the beautiful scripture, The Lord's song and explain to her how Arjuna in his confusion and dilemma had surrendered himself to Krishna's Lotus Feet and had asked Him to tell him how he could face the most difficult situation in his life. Hemlata, being an intelligent girl, immediately connected the condition of Arjuna's despair with her own condition and asked Krishna for guidance, surrendering herself at His Lotus Feet.

Anuradha told Hemlata that she should trust the Lord and keep reading the Bhagwad Gita diligently to get all the answers she sought. Anuradha felt relieved and looked around for Mrityaa's reassuring presence and sure enough, Mrityaa was nearby and gave Anuradha a beautiful smile. That day, her mission was accomplished and Anuradha came home to her wonderful husband. “How was your day sweetheart”? asked Krishna and Anuradha just gave him a tight hug in answer. Sometimes they did not need to talk, they both just understood each other. Anuradha slept peacefully that night.

CHAPTER ELEVEN

MEENA PATTI 'S STORIES OF LOSS AND LOVE

Your children are not your children. They are the sons and daughters of Life's longing for itself. They come through you, but not from you, And though they are with you yet they belong not to you. You may give them your love but not your thoughts, For they have their own thoughts. You may house their bodies but not their souls, For their souls dwell in the house of tomorrow, Which you cannot visit, not even in your dreams. You may strive to be like them, but seek not to make them like you. For life goes not backward nor tarries with yesterday. You are the bows from which your children as living arrows are sent forth.- Kahlil Gibran In The Prophet

While all these stories were going on, and Anuradha was busy helping people who were crossing over to the other side, one morning she woke up, and in her meditation, she saw her beloved grandmother, Meena Patti. Anuradha had loved her grandmother very dearly and she was showered with love by her in her childhood days.

Her grandmother had passed on, when Anuradha was in College, at nineteen years of age. That beautiful morning, Meena Patti appeared in Anuradha's meditation and related the story of her life to her. Anuradha had heard these stories when she was a little girl but at that young age, they had not made that kind of impact on her. Now she understood the meaning of her beloved grandmother's stories of loss and unconditional love. Meena Patti was a wonderful young lady married to Vaidyanathan Thatha and they both had migrated from Kerala when Patti was only 15 years old.

They were very young and very much in love. They had dreams of living a beautiful life in the city of dreams, Bombay. They were fine, except for the fact that they did not know the place and the language at all, they only spoke Tamil and Malayalam. But Meena Patti was a born fighter and was determined to succeed in this alien land. She also had a flair for languages and started learning, Hindi, Marathi and Gujrati all at the same time. She was a kind, compassionate soul and helped all her neighbours in whatever way she could. People loved her and reached out to her in their times of trouble.

They called her Mamiji and consulted her for any problem. She could also read and write English, which made her a valuable asset to the community where she lived. Both Thatha and Patti were very fond of children and had hopes of having their own children some day and of raising a beautiful family. Soon, Patti became pregnant and both of them were overjoyed.

The day dawned bright and beautiful when they held their beautiful baby boy in their arms, he was the most perfect baby they had ever seen and both fell in love with him immediately. Patti took care of little Kartik and nursed him tenderly, the baby started growing little by little. In a month's time, he was a little bigger than when he was born.

To their great misfortune, Bombay was afflicted with an epidemic of cholera. Many small babies developed the deadly infection and died within a few days. Little Kartik was also one of them. Thatha and Patti were devastated. Their little bundle of joy was taken away from them before he could even start his life. They cried inconsolably for many days and eventually found the courage to face life, because their love gave them hope and joy. They found great strength in each other and resumed their life with gratitude in their hearts to the Lord, for He had taken away their baby, but showered them with His love which they found in each other.

Meena Patti was a melodious singer and sang in many languages, invariably she sang songs of praise to the Lord. She found great solace now in her time of grief, to remember the Lord and thank Him for His mercies. Thatha was not religious, though he was highly Spiritual. He wondered about the strange ways of the Universe and was content to rest in His Kindness, happily allowing his lovely wife to pray formally. They complemented each other and dealt with the grief of losing their first born.

Little did they know that the Lord had planned more tragedies for them. After a year, Meena Patti was pregnant again and this time she was absolutely delighted. She was also very careful, avoiding any kind of danger, staying home most of the time and taking good care of her health. This time, she delivered a baby girl, but alas, the child was still born.

In those times, this was a common occurrence, though nobody knew the reason and could do nothing about it. After a full-term pregnancy, hope filling every waking moment and after losing one baby, and getting a baby girl, but losing her on delivery itself, was a painful experience to say the least. Both Thatha and Patti felt as if a part of them was gone and were silent in their grief this time. They did not speak anything for many months and the joy seemed to have gone from their life forever.

The next time she conceived, Meena Patti underwent an abortion when the foetus was 3 months old, so this time, they had not even seen their baby and it was too small to have an independent existence. The grief in their life was unbearable by now, all hope for starting a family, leaving them for a long time to come. It was at this time that, Meena Patti's cousin visited them from the village. She was sister whom Patti loved dearly. The lady had married a year after Meena Patti and had a little baby girl. She had decided to migrate to Bombay with her husband and baby and landed up at Thatha and Patti's doorstep one fine morning, knowing that she would be welcome anytime.

Thatha and Patti were the most generous souls and never refused anyone their hospitality and care. The sisters were overjoyed to meet each other after so many years and Thatha and Patti gladly accommodated the family till they could find a job and afford a home of their own. Their daughter Jayanti was a little darling, chubby and bubbling with energy and enthusiasm. She had just learnt to speak and would talk non-stop. This event changed Thatha and Patti's life forever. They started smiling again and the joy came back to fill their home, in the form of this little Angel.

Krishna has ways of bringing interest back into people's lives just when everything seems hopeless and dark. Meena Patti started singing again and was happy to teach little Jayanti her beautiful songs. Days, weeks and months passed. The couple finally found their feet and moved out of Thatha and Patti's home to their own residence.

It was a happy parting though and left Thatha and Patti with new hope for making yet another attempt to start their own family. Fortune favours the brave and this time, things were favourable for Anuradha's beloved grandparents. They were blessed with a beautiful baby girl. she was a lovely child and was born into a loving home, wining her parents' heart with her mere presence.

Life took on a beautiful turn and it was a joyous time for them all. The baby grew fast and started occupying her parents time and energy. They doted on her and made her happy with their unconditional love and care. They named her Vijaya, their victorious One. Vijaya was a gentle and loving soul. And Anuradha's grandparents were so grateful for the gift of her that they never said a harsh word to her.

The family was cheerful, happy, joyous and absolute bliss filled their beings. They ate their simple meals together and Meena Patti sang joyfully, teaching little Vijaya all her beautiful melodies. The Mother and daughter were inseparable. The father and daughter adored each other with an ardent devotion. Life was a blessing.

To add to their joys, my grandparents were blessed with Anuradha's Father, 5 years after they had her Aunt. By then grandfather had entered his forties and grandmother was in her thirties. They could not believe their great good fortune, when the nurse announced that they had been blessed with a baby boy. It was time for God to take them out of their sorrows, and make up for all the difficult days.

Anuradha remembered her Aunt and Father as the most loving brother and sister duo. They never argued and supported each other through thick and thin. It was all because her grandparents showered all their love on them and love is all there is. Life becomes a song when love is the basis of one's family and one speads that love to all. Anuradha remembered what her grandmother used to say about bringing up children.

She would tell Anuradha how precious children are and how much she had longed for her own child. "Children are like flowers, we must always bring them up with tender loving care", Meena Patti would say. "We must never hurt them with harsh words, even if they make a mistake, instead we must teach them lovingly", she would say.

Both her grandparents did just that, Anuradha knew because her Father and Aunt were the proof of that fact, they never fought and spread their parents' love to all around them. Anuradha felt happy after seeing her beloved grandmother and listening to her story in her meditation. It was now time for her to be moving on, and being connected to her grandparents, her beloved Father and her Aunt gave her a lovely sense of belonging.

She would be meeting all these blessed souls and her own Mother after she left her body. This gave Anuradha a blissful feeling and she told her husband about it while they had their morning tea.

He was happy for her and also recalled his own parents and the fact that he would be meeting them too, once they left their bodies. Joy and anticipation filled their hearts as they waited for Mrityaa to carry them over to the Magical Lands which awaited them.

CHAPTER TWELVE

MERGED WITH KRISHNA FOREVER

The path of love is narrow. It cannot accommodate two. When I was there, He was not. And there is nothing now but He. - Kabir

Anuradha reached home with Mrityaa. She felt happy to be in her husband's arms at the end of the tiring day. They hugged each other for what appeared to be an eternity. They were close to the end of their earthly sojourn. "How many more hours do we have, Mrityaa?" asked Anuradha. "Tonight and the day tomorrow," said Mrityaa. "Thank you, my darling," said Anuradha. "Can you leave us alone, tonight?" teased Anuradha. "Of course, Maa," Mrityaa grinned.

After Mrityaa left, they stared at each other happily. "Let's sing our favorite songs," said Krishna. Anuradha played the karaoke and the couple sang to their hearts content through the night. Dawn came, spreading its pink across the sky. It felt like the heavens were celebrating.

Anuradha made two cups of cinnamon tea, which they sat sipping as they witnessed the beautiful sunrise. Krishna called their daughter and their two sons. "We are going on a long tour," he said. "Come over in the evening to say your farewells." The children came over with their spouses and children. Later, everyone would recall how radiant the couple looked on the day. Mrityaa came as night fell. Anuradha and Krishna held each other and looked at the sky.

There, in the depths of the sky, they were blessed with a vision of Lord Krishna, their chosen form for worshipping the one the celestials had called Many God. "We are leaving our bodies," announced Krishna. "Don't be alarmed or sad for us. Lord Krishna is here to take us home." The children looked on anxiously. There were tears in their eyes. They knew they were witnessing something extraordinary. True to his promise, the Lord had appeared to take them home.

The couple brought their palms together and chanted: Hare Krishna Hare Krishna Krishna Krishna Hare Hare Hare Rama, Hare Rama Rama Rama Hare Hare The couple took a deep breath and closed their eyes. Their bodies fell limply on the sofa.

CHAPTER THIRTEEN

ON DYING CONSCIOUSLY

Whatever one experiences in between two bodies is the result of one's own deeds both good and evil.- Mahabharata of Vyasa

Birth is the emerging from a womb of a body animated by the power of soul. Death is the state where the physical body formed of matter ceases to be animated by the soul.

The Bhagvad Gita, declares that the wise grieve neither for the dead nor for the living. The body is material (made of matter or the five elements). The soul is non-material (comprising 'stuff' that is not subject to sickness, aging or death). There is neither birth nor death for the soul. The soul has for eternity expressed itself through one body after another in a cycle that knows neither beginning nor end.

For the individual soul, the law of karma and consequence rules the trajectory of this cycle of birth and death. The third eternal reality is God. In the Vedic view, matter, soul and God are uncreated. They have always been and they will always be. The human birth is considered special by the wisdom traditions of India because it is man alone of all animals who has the potential to realize while being in the physical body of these three realities – God, Man and Matter.

To know about these three experientially and their relationships with each other is the goal of all spiritual practice in the Indian wisdom traditions. The one who has reached the state of realization of the three disparate yet intertwined realities is no longer buffeted by the waves of bondage to the body, which follows the pattern of karma consequence-karma-consequence. Such a person is said to have died consciously to ordinary bodily existence.

The scriptures tell us that a person who has arrived at a state of such profound awareness is said to possess the gift of choosing his/her time of death. Such souls exit the Earth at will. Death inspires fear; in fact, all fear is ultimately the fear of death. There is, however, the question: Is death the end of the mind, body or soul or all of these? The body is a combination of the five elements: earth, air, water, fire and ether. When the body dies, it stops functioning. The heart stops beating, the breathing stops and the body becomes lifeless. What is the mind? It is a collection of thoughts/ memories/ emotions that run continuously through the brain.

The mind dies with the body. What is the soul? Does it die when the body dies? No, it does not! The soul is consciousness. It never dies. It expresses itself as life in the body. When the soul 'leaves' the body or stops expressing itself through the body, the soul doesn't get destroyed. It folds itself back into the Source/ God, which is its true home. Some say the soul and the Source are non-dual (not-two), others say they are One, and there are also those who say they are non dual but different simultaneously like the fire and the sparks that spring from that fire.

In this understanding, the soul and the Super Soul are One but different. Even the body made of matter is not destroyed in the essential sense; it merely transforms from one form to another. The mind dies too as it is a part of body. The soul, however, lives on. God is but an acronym for the Grand Overall Design. He is not just the Maker, but One who has left His fingerprints on all he has created so we may like detectives know Him. It is God alone who has become the movie that is the world and all souls are enthralled with the action on the screen; death is but an interval before the movie resumes. All spiritual practice is the journey from our screens to the Divine Projector.

On realizing that we are merely being entertained by impressions/ illusions/ insubstantial images, the movie ceases to hold us in its thrall. The thing is that we are not merely watching the movie; we are playing roles in it driven by our desires. After we realize that it is all make believe, the movie continues for others but we do not respond to it emotionally as we did earlier when we mistakenly believed it was real.

Such a soul refuses to delay death when it comes. Even the desire to take birth again dies because what is the point of being despondent or ecstatic while playing a role in a play/ a movie. Such a soul remains with the Source as it refuses to participate in any more plays directed by the Source. It is pack up time! Given these realities, what is the point of fearing death?

Fear comes with the identification with the body, and the belief that it is real. The character we are playing, as we inhabit a particular body dies and we drop the body and start in a fresh body in another birth as the divine director says: lights, camera, and action! So, then, this is how you go about the business of embracing your own mortality.

Make peace with the Grand Overall Design. This helps you accept that life and death are equally part of the Grand Design. The soul never dies, so your near and dear one has not really left completely. You can if you wish receive non-verbal messages from the soul if you are keen on connecting with it. The messages may come to you through people if you are open to it. You may also choose to just send peaceful vibrations to your loved one and tell them you are fine and that they have your good wishes for their onward journey to the Source as they leave your physical presence.

Going back to the Source is the journey Home from space-time to the infinitely loving, peaceful and joyful Source. It is the most beautiful event that can ever be imagined. We are happy when a baby is born. We should treat death as a celebration where a soul is returning to the Source.

CHAPTER FOURTEEN

DON'T GRIEVE TOO MUCH

It is totally understandable that you will miss the physical presence, the sight, sound and hugs with your loved one. But allowing this grief to take over completely will actually sadden the departed soul because that soul can now read your mind and will be aware of your feelings. It will make it more difficult for that soul to cross over and go to the Source completely. So it is better to let the soul embark on its journey. It is like allowing our children to move out of home when they grow up and live their own life.

YOU WILL ALWAYS BE CONNECTED

Remember that the soul never dies. You will always be connected to your loved one, even if you can't see him or her or touch him or her or can't talk to them. Just keep them in your mind and message them mentally. They are still present and you are connected with them through the Source. So your connection with God allows you to connect with your near and dear ones. Never feel lonely because they are not with you, they keep helping you in so many ways.

If you are observant, you will get a hundred signals from your loved ones that help you in your journey. You will feel happy and loved when you think about them. The moment your heart experiences that person's soul, it connects to that soul and you feel peaceful warmth spreading in your heart, telling you that they are there with you, holding your hand every moment. Difficulties in your life disappear and life becomes easier for you because your loved one is telling the Source to help you remove your obstacles.

KNOW THAT DEATH APPEARS TO BE FINAL BUT IS NOT THE END

Death is like us changing clothes. The soul changes bodies but is imperishable. So death looks final, but is not so. It is an opportunity for that soul to get a brand new body with new parents and new opportunities to fulfill their desires and be happy. So it is certainly a beautiful gift for that soul. For the ones who are left behind, it appears final, but it is only a temporary separation. If you really want to be with your loved one beyond death and invite them back into your life, they come back as a newborn child. You are sure to connect with that soul again, if both of you desire so. It is not a final separation.

There are so many examples of souls who come back on Earth and remember their previous lives. Maybe that soul forgets, because that is the design by God, for the soul to forget the previous life, but the souls who remain on Earth recognize the soul immediately. Isn't it an exciting that you can reconnect with souls despite temporary separations caused by death? Death is only a temporary interruption. It is never spells the end for really strong relationships.

CHAPTER FIFTEEN

DEATH IS NOTHING TO BE FEARED

Understanding death makes us strong beyond anything we can imagine. It gives us the confidence to live life completely every moment. It frees us of fear forever. Everybody who is born on earth has to die. Being a part of the Grand Overall Design, this cannot be avoided but it can certainly be understood.

After understanding it, fear of death leaves you once and for all because ignorance is the root cause of fear. Death is an exciting opportunity for a soul to leave an old, diseased body and acquire a new one. It is an opportunity provided by God to a soul to fulfill its material desires. If you want to find love, you are sure to find it. If you want riches and a luxurious life, you will get it for sure.

If you want a great education and be a learned person, it is all possible. Death is an excellent opportunity to start all over again. It is not the end but a new beginning. And for those who understand this Grand Overall Design, death is a final liberation, from the repeated cycles of birth and death. For them, death is the final homecoming. It is a Grace beyond all Grace, because it is the final merging of our individual soul (jivatman) with the Universal Soul

(Paramatman).

Can such a homecoming inspire fear? Can there be a greater joy? Think about it. Death completes the circle that begins at death. Death gives what even life can never give, a sense of completion, a sense of fulfillment.

CHAPTER SIXTEEN

BE PREPARED FOR DEATH AT ALL TIMES

Mortals do not know when death will come. The fact that it can come the next instant is what makes life beautiful. We also have to consider the possibility that the people we love, all our dear ones, our parents, our children or our friends, may be taken from us at any instant.

We have to accept that death can strike anyone. It is very much in the realm of possibility. It is likely that we will live to see our parents die. Children are lost to accidents, suicide or disease.

We need to prepare for such deaths too. Being prepared for such deaths helps us deal with the pain when it comes to us. Surrounding our selves with people who have a patient ear, a compassionate heart and a spiritual outlook helps. It follows that we have to awaken these latent qualities in our selves so we can comfort others who are grieving.

It is important we develop a spiritual outlook starting today. It is equally important that literature, teachers and communities that disseminate such an outlook reach people around you as immediately as possible because a grieving person may not be in a condition to absorb any knowledge if the shock has been too traumatizing.

In such a case it is a great service just to be there for the person unobtrusively and encourage them to talk about the person. You may also express gratitude for the departed person and talk about how the person had contributed to your life.

It is not a time to offer advice unless it is explicitly sought. Be respectful, compassionate and loving. We conclude by recalling the Latin phrase – Memento Mori or remember death – and its relationship with yet another phrase in the same language – Carpe Diem or seize the day. It is only the reality of death, which makes it imperative upon us that we 'seize' the present day, the glittering, shining procession of present moments that we have been granted, and make the most of them.

Death is certain!
Live!

Epilogue– Beyond The End

Death is not an end. It is a doorway. Throughout Mrityaa, you may have searched for answers—about life, loss, fear, purpose. But the truth is, death takes nothing away. It reveals. What we truly are cannot be destroyed. What we fear is often what we do not understand.

If this book has done anything, let it be this: To make you pause... To make you question...To make you live more consciously. Because in understanding death, we finally begin to understand life.

Key Reflections from Mrityaa

Death is not the opposite of life—it is part of it. Fear dissolves when awareness deepens. The body ends, but consciousness continues. Every ending is a transformation. Living fully is the only way to transcend death.

A Letter To The Reader

Dear Reader,

If you've reached here, you didn't just read this book—you experienced it. You may have felt discomfort, curiosity, maybe even resistance. That is natural. Mrityaa is not meant to comfort—it is meant to awaken. Ask yourself: Am I truly living, or just existing? What am I afraid to face? If today were my last day, what would matter? Let these questions stay with you. Because the purpose of this book was never to give you answers—but to help you discover your own.

Gratitude

To life—for its unpredictability.
To death—for its certainty.
To every experience that shaped this understanding.
And to you, for being open enough to read this.

If this book resonated with you: Reflect daily on your mortality—not with fear, but awareness. Journal your thoughts about life and death. Engage in silence and self-inquiry. Share this perspective with those ready to listen. Because awareness grows when it is shared. One day, everything you see will fade. But what you become... will remain. So live in such a way that when death arrives, it does not feel like an end— but a return.

With awareness,
– The Authors

About The Authors

The authors of Mrityaa are seekers who question life beyond the surface. Through experiences, observations, and deep reflection, this book emerged as an exploration of one of the most misunderstood truths: death. Rather than seeing it as darkness, the author invites you to see it as clarity.

Dr. Anuradha Iyer is a professor and Head of Department in Physiology at SHK Government Medical College, Mewat, Haryana. She has a keen interest in yoga, bhakti, and Vedanta traditions. She is also the author of the book Krishnapriya, a fictional account of a devotee's search for Lord Krishna.

Satish Purohit is a writer, editor, book reviewer, and author coach. His professional background spans journalism, publishing, editing, writing, and bookselling. He has provided professional value to brands such as Mumbai Mirror, Times of India Group, Mid-Day, Indian Express, FressPress Journal, Granth Book Store, Cross Word Bookstores, and Life Positive Magazine.

Mamta Shah is a painter, illustrator, and Art Teacher based in Gurgaon.

www.ingramcontent.com/pod-product-compliance
Lightning Source LLC
LaVergne TN
LVHW090329210926
848480LV00004B/1347